The Dedalus Press

Down in the Deeper Helicon

John Ennis

"And voices singing . . . .
. . . .
. . . .
These fragments I have shored against my ruins".

T. S. Eliot, *The Wasteland*

DOWN IN THE DEEPER HELICON

JOHN ENNIS

DUBLIN

The Dedalus Press
24 The Heath,
Cypress Downs,
Dublin 6W
Ireland

ISBN 1 873790 60 0(paper)
ISBN 1 873790 61 9 (bound)

Cover painting by Jane O'Malley

for Ann, my children and friends

Acknowledgements are made to the editors of the following publications where some of these poems, or versions of them, were first published: *Poetry Ireland Review; Humanitas; Initials; Toward Harmony, A Celebration for Tony O'Malley; The Waterford Review, The Remnant.*

Dedalus Press Books are represented and distributed abroad by Password, 23 New Mount St., Manchester M4 4DE.

Printed in Ireland by Colour Books Ltd.

The Dedalus Press receives financial assistance from An Chomhairle Ealaíon, The Arts Council, Ireland.

CONTENTS

The Nearer Obsequies

This Church that is Stripped Down

THE BANNOW DAYS

"day after day stringing us through
the ordinary this house has learned to keep"

Dave Smith, *Graduation*

REFLEXOLOGY

Let us make love then, talk of simple things,
The deeds you did today, what you had to eat,
What you think tomorrow and the day after bring.
I will sit back, caress your tender feet.

There will be enough talk to fill in forever.
We will go on talking into the liquid night.
If I rest my head on you, it will not be for love's fever
But because I grow weak, hungry on love's diet :

For from you is all my food and my drink,
Play me more of the songs I've never heard.
Without them I can't stand, or hope, or think.
These Songs of Songs are family, every word.

And love me, again, I beg you, you must
Or my dry soul will give up, turn to dust.

COFFEE JARS

How many words of affection have we
Not spoken yet, spun through our lips, countless
As sands, yet commensurate with sea
Dunes, where seagrasses stretch off boundless

Into our futures with sea thrift, hollies, kidney vetch,
Smell of salt and combers and the white of froth
Of oceans, and the spray of storms that stretch
The mind, rack hearts, merely emphasise the depths of both?

Yes, those words we've spoken in our mutual care,
They are not insignificant, have begun great dunes
Where the loves of half Waterford were conceived for a dare,
Tenderness was whispered to the latest transistor tunes

In the snatched heats of summer. Our grassy hearts are calm
Today, threaded with root fibres, attachments, tendrils of marram.

AUGUST RENOVATIONS

Not Wordsworth's country, but it might well be,
These grounds round Tintern Abbey on the Bannow.
The venerable beeches at the entrance, tree by tree,
Stand like sentinels for our Tintern of the Vow.

Here doves frequent the ancient battlements
And today's scaffolding that makes them good
While swallows dart to and fro in their element
Above the corbels and the vaulted aisles.
          One enjoys new wood,

Elm. Pride of restoration. And I see, again, our clear outline
(Though bunged up by useless brick and the debris of years)
Yes, custom and Cistercian-like, the ceremony of the routine
Renewed with purity of forms and, maybe, an end to tears.

We've seen the ghosts of shipwreck, of Mareschal, in the tide.
And so we renew our vows, while time is on our side.

INITIALS

The years have built their cities below our eyes,
Daubed their graffiti on the chipboard of the mind.
We have become walled-in slaves to our families
Hours, days, weeks, months. Years gone on our kind.

You have problem veins. All the rearing.
Who once had the finest legs in Ardkeen.
Reduced before your time with the caring,
And still there's no end to it can be seen.

So we undress humbly now by our B & B bed
Close to the gates of Tintern, know in our bones
The dissolution, and the fears, that lie ahead.
We have seen ourselves at twilight in the stones,

Who have gathered each into the other's embrace
These twenty-one years. Your questions now buffet
        my corbelled face.

GRATITUDE

Eating ripe melon at 4.45am near Tintern,
I scoop it to the last and each alternate spoon
We share and slake our thirst with and earn
The other's gratitude. I open a window to the moon

Breathe in the scented August air. During this last hour
We sprang to each other at a breakneck pace
Plumbed, and replumbed, familiar depths with power
Incarnate, together, like on a Grecian vase.

And we went back to a resplendent time.
We had not even met, there was no talk of marriage
Or honeymoons, children; we existed in a tender dream
Of what might be. We were a third of our age.

I took you to the spacious heights and there you knew no fears.
You caressed me through places I haven't been for years.

TOURNIQUET

So hard, why do we each clasp the other's hand
So hard these few days we can call our own
On coastal streets that are pedestrianised, and bland
By turn, on every beach, in every park we visit or have known?

There is an urgency I can't put a name to
Each time we separate, or come back to a queue.
The red tidal blood is ebbing out of view.
Our fingers move to provide a tourniquet.

For there is a calmness that belies despair:
The confident stride, the bearing in one's talk,
While all around there is a coming up for air,
Just one more time, with people, as they walk.

I will not be the one, dear flame, to let you go
Till these knuckles purple, this palm's as cold as snow.

OVER BENN'S BRIDGE

"Life is the building of bridges
Over rivers that seep away"
Gottfried Benn

I have attempted bridges, pontoons where I can
And seen them all washed away with daily floods.
They fight and die for me, my children, to a man
Carried away by deluges, secretions, now by words.

The army that marches in me grows more desperate
To force a bond forever across the swollen rivers,
To join the tie of earth to earth, defeat the muddy spate
That would see all endeavour doomed, induce fevers'

Final coldness. Strip to the wintry, arthritic bone.
And I that should command my mind, cannot.
Days pass like centuries. More battles lost than won.
We cry out in reeds to one another. Distraught,

Come, with one push more, we'll reach the other side.
The meadows of lost species, where we can nest and hide.

TURBULENCE

I had thought to show you wild bluebells in the wood
But they have blown now in May's threshing storms.
I had thought to show you the flowering sycamores,
Southern gales blew their honeyed iron away from us.

I had thought to show you the creamed and fragrant thorn
But its white petals litter the younger weeds and grass.
I had thought to show you the scented half-hidden rowan
But its innocence for this year will be lost to our nostrils.

I had thought to walk you through innumerable white apples
With the bees you fear clambering them for nectar and pollen.
I had thought we might stop awhile by Grieve and by Pippin
Where your eyes would have opened to another genesis.

I had thought without reference to beginnings, and so planned.
Now must wrestle with chaos in my own back garden.

DEEP PLOUGHING

We plough familiar ground again and it is good,
The clay pliant, rising with us, free from stone.
All the stubborn and sock-rending rocks are gone.
Here's one love of many to be seen to, to warm the blood

On a winter's day when the storm rises over the wood.
The south-east gale still has the dry cold sting
Of continental Europe where snows are settling.
I am a man reborn and feel all that is good

In your arms up and down the ash bole,
The beech trunk, and the naked sycamore,
That stand by us as we wait on, as if for evermore,
Erect and leafless for the explosive green growth of the soul.

Then let the sleet and the mist and the darkness descend.
We'll wing our cries above them till the end.

HELICON,

MUSE COUNTRY 1

"To see myself, to set the darkness echoing."

Seamus Heaney, *Personal Helicon*

SINKING WELLS

You open up in me the deeper springs.
These come now welling cold and pristine to the surface.
Deeper loams come first, pale soft sands, way-out imaginings.
The rounded pebbles, then, where subterranean dreams meet,
      interface.

Once I sunk a well and the well sunk me.
I went into debt over it for years, could not
Pipe its iron and lucid goodness within for my family.
The fruit of my expenditure was set at naught.

But, today, your goodness is on tap all round.
I bring a new comfort to all my kind,
Embrace each for his, or her own worth, find,
And lay down for them the old greatcoat of my affection
      on the ground.

Diviner of diviner kind,
You've made to gush the purer fountains of my mind.

ARTESIAN

Yes, though it sank me, I sank the well.
Five hundred pounds you cost. Today the piping's
Capped with a cement block, where waters weave a spell,
Criss-cross, caress cold pebbles down in depth-trodden springs.

I paid the Wexford Walls, leaders in the field,
Or reputed so, to go one hundred and seventy feet
Down so rife is pollution, three times the clayey plummet
Of old midland wells. My lot's artesian now, not to yield.

I would avoid the chlorine-cliched reservoir
Whose light ricochets a sick orange on the grey November mist.
Trespassers read the warnings. Is it in vain, this deeper bore?
I would have you flow within my house. You that none can resist.

One day I'll draw transparence from you, pure and passion cold
From the great depths of what is to be, until we, too, grow old.

AFTER EMILY

The day will come when I'll rise, seek out my kind
Drink from the fountains that made us what we are.
I will know no fear that day, but a joy unconfined
As I did once when as a boy I laid my soul bare,

Wept away the falsity in another's words.
My kind will be select, uncontrollably One.
I will pour out my mouth again, speak the cry of birds
Lost in a wilderness. I will be understood by anyone

Who has a countenance not turned to stone.
Or maybe you, too, will stare me down hard and long.
Some will set me up on a pedestal I do not own.
Others will sing my words, who never knew my song.

If my words cut deeper, now, into your bone,
It's human warmth I seek. Marrow like my own.

ORPHEUS DISMEMBERED

And know I will never grow ashen cold to you
Or only till this heart has stopped an hour or two,
Rests en route if donated; also, if my eyes will do
A favour, the heart, the lungs, the warm kidneys, too –

And even if all of these are severed, and are gone,
One last Orphic miracle, if only my lips could move,
Yes, this cooled remnant will somehow summon up love's monotone
And my breathless affection I will, voiceless, once more prove.

For, if ever I appear cool, it's only a dawn hoar
Frost on some poor bare Etna, or Vesuvius, you see.
Do not ever doubt the lava ready in my deepest core
I keep the hard crust on for too long an eternity.

Thus, denuded in the flames, I'll commend my way to you.
Brother Furnace, enliven my tongue, everything I do.

Construct me no shibboleths, no memorial
Column, ring me no bell, or write homilies to grace
The mouth; neither is text to hang on a white wall
Or sculpture, blank, bland, angular and useless.

You give me back my name, my tongue. You call
To me from far shores that are shores no more,
Rather dust, poor interstellar dusts, unequal
Hopes long unknown to the last soul or its core.

We chose in each other, once, the greater seam
And this will never be wrested away from us.
We have seen for all time the constant gleam.
Our endless days are instant, industrious.

I would have known your inspiration while there was still time.
You scatter me in fervent ash while I am in my prime.

MUSE 2

I am tearing apart at the seams
And much stupidity fills my day.
Yet I see mirages only, paper streams,
Mirages the more I near them the further they slip away.

The old and perfect form, that is renewed,
That is made molten for a joint enterprise
Harbours my entrails and their half-digested food.
Poetry must be alive and vital. Masticating to the eyes.

And I would have you speak to me some more.
If I drown at dawn, what good is a lifejacket at noon?
I hardly ever see you round my door.
Christ, your garden might be on Pluto. Or the moon.

When a friend last saw O'Riada, the composer said, "Mairim".
Promises. Promises on leaves. I read them all the time.

MUSE 3

A thousand consummations I have known,
Or yet not known, if one enjoins pure ecstasy
As the criterion. True lyricism in the bone
Marrow, with a kindred theme, isn't easy.

Maybe it is impossible on this side
Of eternity where the human species
Must procreate, go about its needs, decide
Who'll bed whom. Rhymes, it seems, decide issues.

Yet when I speak to you, or call your name,
I kneel to that creative shudder in the thighs
Which never was, but is toward which we aim.
You must not think of this as mere poetic lies.

For if you find no consummation in my lines,
It's early days yet in genesis. Read the signs.

MAGMA MOTHER

I've given You the earth's molten lava.
You've seen it stream off down my slopes
Searing, burning, flaming this tiny Rakata off Java –
Then crust, harden, grow cold just like old hopes

Can, do congeal. Soul, if I call it such
Or that part of me that wells up eternal
In image, word, and the thought of touch,
Is similar in essence, capable of torching all

Hopes and flowers, the vines we'd sow together.
But will my small Krakatoa really darken your world?
My debris cloud the sun for years? Bring us foul weather?
I doubt it. Get off my back, you squinting eunuchs or be forever
     hurled :

But You, Mother, visit me soon in my deepest core.
You will know more, then, of what I have in store.

WITH THE OLD MASTERS

He questioned softly "Why I failed?"
"For Beauty," I replied –
"And I – for Truth – Themself are One –
We Brethren, are." He said –

Emily Dickinson, *449*

"They were professionals; they lived in fire."

Vincent Buckley, *Lament for the Makers*

AENGUS ON ARAN

1

Morning, and I head out to Aran, the old disarray,
Climb up to your ocean-spattered battlements, Aengus.
Herds of the young eat the cheerless gruel of the day,
Shout for more from the palm of the stone god that feeds us.

The keen wolfhounds howl shut in stone. On the grey
Rock the grassroots hang on for the signal to rise, the word
Of hope. Hundreds of us rot down in the seal-dead bay.
Claws on the Atlantic floor attempt the bitter chord.

Stone. Bronze. Iron. We pass on. Tears of the infant.
Your cauldron fires are in ash. Gold, glass and metallurgy
Fail. Wood dwindles. We forage stone for roots, the edible plant.

Cliffs, to the sunset, drop sheer. Poet, from this height
No retreat is possible. Even the cold demented sea
Licks your hurt in the coinless, unscrupulous light.

2

Yes! Home to the Atlantic! The true salt on our cheeks.
For it is no fluke that here you ordered stone on stone,
Firmed chevaux-de-frize bedrock. Over the future weeks
You'll build of our beleagured wills the final bastion.

The green plains are lost. Your children too. Firbolgs enshrine
The emerald flicker at their fingertips, the robotic gall
Of the breadline. Industry opens with cheese and wine,
Cuts the tape on the door of rock for the hounded animal.

Sailing west, you settled for extremity. With eyes of pride
You chose this last outpost. Boys stand armed; two mend a net.
In the damp cantankerous dawn the wives scold and chide.

We'll fish from dizzy limits down into the low red sunset.
Sea foam drifts like snow in winter on Aran at high tide.
Skins walk on us, grow lousy. People shiver, mate in the wet.

3

Mount the sentries! Coin hoarders of ordure and slim ease
School the Croms of the boyish fields, would make us kneel
To them. Aengus! Impossible! Though we know no release,
House us with polity and poems to quieten the desolate seal.

Friends didn't make this far. The best fell in oaken bogs
    with the dead acorn
Seeds. With cottony bog-scraws we covered their last stare.
Expect snow falling early on the cuddled generations,
    those not yet born
And on love, new lovers, cradled to breathe clean air.

Fine. We'll perfect seacraft, sail white breakers in the rain
Snatch soil from mainland crevices to pluck the yearly morsel,
Filch eggs from the screaming gulls to ease the pain;

Wait on the moon-lit ramparts. Construct the twelve-foot wall
Into immortality maybe. I fear wild summers we cannot haul
The threshing blue sharks in, much less boil liver, extract the oil.

ENVOI

Our lamps are going out. Fear rages. Rage steels us under this sky
On this rock. There remains the ocean with gulls, geese,
    fish to get by.
Soon the last wave. Guide us, Wandering Aengus,
    into a new strategy.

CELT

And if you'd ever see me now so vulnerable again,
I pray it will be like my ancient friend, the Dying Gaul
Hand on a wounded thigh, who knows deepest pain,
Sinking slowly down, who once with stamina stood tall,

Whose art had the Yeatsian sword to make it talk,
Whose proud arteries flow on with blood in bronze and stone,
Who cannot now get to his feet or walk:
The one whom Attalos honoured when all hope had gone.

That torc of gold, I thought it harboured me
And you, who must ever look the pit in the face,
Accept in the side the spear of begrudgery.
But you and I will never let them call out our names in disgrace

Though left, none to fight for, none to hang on for, none to pine
For, as we settle slowly separately down together on the earth,
        at last to be supine.

CREATION MOTHER

I've become an eternal burden to prairie and creation,
Like an old snakeskin that should be long sloughed off,
Like an old concept ages past its first inception.
Sick, I'm a burden to my love and to the name of love.

And that is why I ask you, children, rest awhile
Search round for dead branches, twigs, dried grass
And other flammables – No, I can't go on one more mile –
I have known birth and death too long, all things
       that come to pass.

I, your old brave Indian Mother, give you a last command :
Prepare the timber, prepare it well, stacked solid round the base;
Smear what grease you can spare on wood, what is to hand
And help me up on the pile. Steady me now, just in case –

And strike the flame gently and let the first smoke rise.
I'll wrap the blanket well about me, wipe the perspiration
       from my eyes.

THE BERRYMAN PIECES

BERRYMAN FALLING

When I see the autumn rowan tree I think of
Berryman, that last ungainly fall and that wave
Of his to the pre-dawn revellers as he fell to ice.
None was to hand, then, to wipe up his final mess.

Collected Poems, rich wing-feed, weighed him down on the bridge;
Henry, bones, thoughts crimsoning like first berries at the edge
Of streams. Astride the viaduct of his Mississippi,
He leaped from dark to turbulent dark with little felicity.

So this appalling absence now leaves us to construe
Symmetries of the leafless void that is in you :
Rush of the last bitter wind that shakes our words
From overburdened trees like fruit for beak-stripping birds.

But it's unlikely we'll ever find the true notes to sing
Your final dull multiple thud, the inevitable fracturing.

BERRYMAN'S FATHER

A holiday morning like any other day
The dawn he shot his heart out in Florida.
You were promised to go to the seaside.
The blast was mostly accurate in the petalled garden.

For that dreadful banker, as you call him, could take no more.
Was your incessant pestering the one final straw?
When I close my ears to a thousand and two orders
I see him go, load with relief the shotgun breach.

It's not easy to extricate ourselves.
The sky may be blue, the birds singing and the sun
Never so pleasant, then the darkness clouds
In the heart, in a flash, in a gasp, in a one-way vision.

I know you wish to spit upon his grave.
Take it easy. Tomorrow's waste attracts its own wave.

HERBERT PARK REVISITED

Berryman, '69, a warm September
I first inhaled your primal joy here.
Even if the leaves were turning
Every nerve cell then in my body
Screamed out, "I am free! I am free!"

Berryman, your Dublin Eden had no peer
– I in my frozen twenties, well, no matter –
(In a corner leaves were burning).
Your white birches, the winter cherry
Had no equal to Bombay.

Berryman, another winter flogs its berries
Links our paths with red cotoneasters.
By December's dark pondwater
I feed the wildfowl, walk my daughter.

HOMAGE TO WANG WEI

Somehow one cannot imagine them –
O'Brudair, Shakespeare or Dante –
Of a morning with a hoe, the dew still damp on the handle in the hand
Limbering up among the roots, a single mistle above on the larch;
Else the empty blue sky and the universe round to yourself.
Not even the ravenous hounds awake yet, and the sun, the sun
A day older, too, struggling onto the mauve Wexford horizon.

ON LEADING THE VERSE EXERCISE:
FROM WANG WEI'S MELON GARDEN c 750

High summer. We young poets surprise him and his yellow orioles.
The old man invites us up the hill with a view of the mountains
Blue to the far south. Pride in his voice; in his step, a waver.
Redundant, on pension from the state, the service of Confucius,
Hiding his poverty. But his melons are coming round their time:
He suggests a verse competition.
The words flow easy
On that slope to the sun, the gold fruit coddled with waxy leaves
A little brittle now, holed with insects, drought and the strain
Of ripening.
Quiet of quills. His hoe is discarded too. Life
Study.
Hsiah Ch'in. I win.

I will scarce be heard of again.

WANG WEI IN OLD AGE

They read with a starker poignancy, the later poems;
The garden acres far beyond all sweat, the willows
Unkempt, your wife long dead, the ageing grey mother
Sunk with the ghosts of your children, and a career, in the dust.

A nausea, your own thinning white hair. But the lute
You were adept at sweeps the water's edge for consolation.
You that were master of painting and poetry and music
See fewer and fewer intimates, the poets from Japan.

That one bosom friend who comes, you talk of walking him
Linked arm in arm to the inevitable boat on the inevitable river
Which curves. You ache to tears. Colours of the evening sky
That know no humanity, you then paint a little warmth into.

On such tepid September evenings, the humming of tired bees
In the ash-leaved pea tree. Lyrics of marauding swallows as they feed.

OUR WILLOWS ARE NOT YOUR WILLOWS

for Wang Wei

I share with you a fondness for the willow.
Gold, green and wild sally grace the garden.
You watched the exiles at the gates of the city
Pulling off tendrils of tears with pliant leaves.

Is this, then, for us all the common state
As inevitable, say, in Confucian China
As here on the barren tarmac of airports;
The same nausea, bog of sickness, at leave times?

The same wild screaming in the ear
The same last minute tearing of limbs
The same turning back, or not at all
And the parent bough nearly stripped.

Till the wound heals over, both body and bole.
Till the resilient willows are again made whole.

JOYCE CYCLING TO OUGHTERARD AND VICO

Consumed. Consumption. What's the difference,
This black pain that racks the chest, the fever and the flame
Engulfing all, decline of all else, for this perishing innocence.
My poems are pebbles thrown toward your bright soul all the same.

I think of Sonny Bodkin down every hollow, over every rise
Chambered at Rahoon, who in the real world
Moulds on at Oughterard, who had a voice.
Stood like a mute Caruso shivering, haunted in the cold.

So great had love's nightly burden become, Michael
Hung on in your back garden, did not want to live.
Look into my eyes too, dear Nora, as well as well
Know the fondness, tenderness of lines I've yet to give

Till I'm young enough again to face the spittle and the blows,
Who may not last, like that boy will, beyond the winter snows.

A CREATION TOO FAR

I had divided ocean from land on a leaf of paper.
I had divided night from day on the back of my hand.
I set stars without number in a cynical firmament.
All this for you, and your children's children.

And, then, you grew by my side to be the gentle master
Counsellor and friend when the famished March blew.
You refashioned from my side the dark girl that loved me.
Like Wisdom, you set down the firm paths I might walk on.

I had set out for you the many seed-bearing plants.
I had set for you the fifty trees with the winged seeds :
I am expended for my love. Whom I love to create.
In whose eyes is gentleness past all understanding.

Each Sunday for you I know no rest from toil.
Exhausted, bone-weary, I rise the seven days.

GIVING A LIFT TO ORPHEUS

Cruising home late from some arts seminar
To do or other, you sat with me in the car.
Regret blinded me for so little done,
How I gave your name to something that won
First prize once at a festival, tidings of a day,
Pale shadow of that vow you eked out of me one May.
I saw you were the more remembered. And that meant
The world. Head of a clan, you had a lyric talent.
And my memorial spieled on sprawling across pages
Heathering an August with its blooms, rough round the edges.
"They do not matter now, our imperfections", your eyes
Comforted. "I said No to the Maenads, walked into Paradise".
Then you were gone. By the Boar's Head I jammed the car brakes
On a few feet from beneath a lorry, saved awhile our twin sakes.

BEYOND THE METAPHYSICAL

I saw eternity, again, the other night
Or what was left of it from his far days,
The man who gazed too in his naked plight,
Addressed a spirit kindred with his ways.

It was a more brutal, yet a clearer, sky
He looked into, that stargazer with love.
He walked his garden with some certainty
He'd be cherished. It was enough.

Enough to fashion a poem of true tenderness
That keeps on falling like a meteorite
All these years to illuminate the stress
Of us, the blind who sense, but do not see, the light

Until it is too late. And our own star, then, and its fever
Are bundled into nothingness forever and forever.

FATHER HOPKINS IN OLD AGE

If You see me creep back into the carapace
That is me, You will know why. The games of care
Are over. If I am on a sheer cliff face
Either help me or let me fall to my despair

Alone for it is better that way, You must agree.
There, once, from my cold and glistening self
I cleansed the bitter grits that bothered me.
I'd confidence I rested on some deeper shelf

Somewhere within You. When I'd reach out, You'd be around.
You've got your universal problems, so have I.
Then, when I needed it the most, the gentle sound
Of Your voice, nothing. My shell broke in the sky

As I went falling, falling, falling. Good friends,
We can talk things over in eternity, when the falling ends.

MICHELANGELO

If You would embrace me once any more
Beware the abyss, then, this sistine emptiness
You might tumble into, too, the silent roar
Of smoky depths I cannot plumb, some call distress.

One says I need help. In this there's token truth.
The human state, perhaps. Julius rests the case
Against me. Subman. Submerged. Hands of ruth
Run mechanical. I add to artifice.

Once upon a time I'd have wept all into Your Shoulder.
Too late. I'm swept away. Much driftwood to contend
With. I'm tired out. There's the odd boulder,
Complication for all. I'm carried to another bend.

Beware, then, this drowning man and his clutch.
Your finger, it is too far distant. All human touch.

WARMING THE REVOLVER BUTT

It is finished. Thunder clouds reciprocate with mine.
It's been that kind, that lack, of day, the indigos
Boiling up toward the unfinished edges,
The crows in industrial black.

Why can't I explore the canvas limits?
Tidy up the craft that little bit more?
Look how the fiery brown earth to the left
Penetrates and is lost in the green of the untrodden!

The cartway bend curves to the infinite.
Only the continents of wheat remain, bright
Gold and opulent in their confusion
The July wind caressing them. Why wait on?

All I've done is wasted another day on the harvesters crouched
With their pipes on the headlands. You grow warm, out of touch.

art Thou there?

Berryman,
Eleven Addresses

If I call out your name, echo it down the years
Make it reverberate in the wild caverns of affection,
Liquidize it in the crush of apples from the garden,
It is, always was, will be sweet music to my ears.

For from it all else, all hope, is derivitive:
The crown, the taproot and the woodland bole,
Leaf, blossom, sepal of the dreaming soul,
Pollen packed and octagonal, the primal hive ...

That you should ask how I am, who am
The powerhouse in the cell, the gathering storm
I celebrate and hold you close in the atom.
I'm the spitting log, the thought that keeps you warm.

Today I saw your sun rise with some permanence.
Your name was written on the dew. Your countenance.

OSCAR IN PARIS

Dear lonely outcast. Everyman. Dear outcast one,
You're seated now by my grave in Parisian gloom.
Your glance would soften even this pitiless stone
To tenderness in the knowing faces round my tomb.

You have so brimmed my broken urn with tears,
You have so gone into me and warmed my mind
The bone side of the marble, and my jailed years,
That your own soul with my love I have lined,

Thus, I entrust you today with Glorious Pity;
See you lead her by the hand fom this grim place,
Talk to Her poor spirits in their houses in one city
After another. Each dawn wake to her embrace.

She charges you daily to hear our fearful cries.
She charges the batteries of the heart. Our empathies.

THE SPIRIT OF THOMAS MANN
CONSIDERS EUROPA

I have seen my crystal affections fall
In honeyed droplets in the penal mirror,
No, not of my years, or some old hackneyed symbol
And yet not with any greater terror

Anymore, or strain to rush to, create new metaphors
But poor naked man not knowing what to do
With all defences down, controls gone, doors
Open, until the end, into the smoky shower like any Jew.

My life has gone for you centrifugal
In the honey extractor, whose revolutions
Are numberless while all my works are finite and frugal.
Release me from this bond. I find no solutions.

For still I load myself into the machine, see
Death, cry out for you as the ripe nectar is swept out of me.

DEVOTEES GATHERING ROUND
JIM MORRISON'S GRAVE

That we would adore You, You took the hammer blows
You found the wood, then were Yourself flung down.
You held the reckless nails. We took off your clothes,
Hoisted You, dear friend, made You a forgotten crown

Of our own sharp devising. And yet You did not cry
Out, banish us with the cold sentence as You might.
And when we plunged the spear beyond your thigh
Only a Merton-like encore filled your inviolate

Eyes. We buried You, unannounced, in a tomb
With inscriptions scrawled like lovers' graffiti.
Till your wild resurrection in us leaves us dumb.
That is why with such awkward affections we

Try to make good to You. Whom we failed. Don't fear
This your darkest hour. Know our embrace is near.

A CREATOR RECONSIDERS

I that have prayed once for oblivion
Now gather in the stars, the building blocks
For one more day, and gather in the rocks
Pinnacled on mountains, then every humble stone –

But, wait a moment, for I've seen your happiness,
And I that break down alone for your great joy
To be, stopped the frenzy of the delinquent boy
Transferred to the farthest spaces all my emptiness.

For such despair has in us no future,
Is alien to every breath we breathe,
Every mote on the sunbeam. We wreathe,
Twin soul, dusts that shimmer in the air.

Our dearest siftings, then, we will ever contain
So that there will be no more sorrow, hurt, or pain.

THE NEARER OBSEQUIES

"It is six months since my father's death
And he has had to endure a deep snow ... "

Thomas McCarthy, *The Sorrow Garden*

THE CORBETSTOWN PIECES

1

THE FOUNTAIN PEN ENTRUSTED

Not in the photograph, but slightly offstage, James,
Your sisters call out to you like three teenage graces,
Watch you toddle across the cropped Offaly pasture
Laughing. Your face is chubby with happiness.

Your mother flickers there in the background,
Holds the Kodak camera, maybe. Her generous throat
Has not yet grown husky after the war.
Cancer has not made advances into her.

Cotton clouds. Sun. Early May. Daisies afoot.
There would be trees over to your right.
Your father has a son.
Gorman, the name, lives on at Corbetstown.

Breda, Carmel and Clare survive in Dublin. James,
You lean on my bed at cockcrow at the end of summer :
Garr school opens a lonely day earlier than Knockaville.
You hold up your mother's pen, use it in her name.

FLIGHT

¡Que no quiero verla!
– Lorca

James

Edenderry
The table with your body
The priest will be sprinkling you now with the prayers
I sit in our Austin A40, refuse to go in

James

Beech trees. Football. Bees in a gable. I visit you over and over
I see you climb with stealth the tall shed wall, whose roof
Blew off with the storm, to catch me the two pigeons
And I stand, cousin, numb, wait in the old happiness

James

ÉSOS ÁRBOLES

The wind in our trees –
Is it still to the good
Or only the memory?

Only I can see
Only I can hear
Individual beech
None else sees.

Do you still smalltalk
High above the pasture
High above the gamespatch
Straggle of nettles under your branches
Stinging our ankles after the ball
In the sparse grazing
Never visited by cattle.

After the auction
Then the emptiness.
One day you went out
The hall door into the field to be shot.
Ambulanced down the lane
Onto the road
Never to return.

Return. Like leaves?
Is it possible?
Or are you felled forever in me and even the very roots wrenched out?

WITH TUTANKAMEN

1

So long
Peace beneath this rubble from the upper tomb of Rameses –
Stones cascading down the flanks of the valley –
Chippings, the tools of workers close by in the stone,
Who have forgotten me in less than a generation
Tapping like twins, once, on the membrane for my fingers
(Just so among the wedding faces move groom and bride
When, for others, our settled plots are dug and shovelled).
Some hot days the occasional larger chunk
Of masonry
With tears of sweat of a labourer of my years falls
       unbeknownst

Amid the songs of valley keeners in see-through costume,
The feasts of the dead with the supple dances of children,
Our packed communal tables, the colourful mealtimes.
We fade like gods of blue granite, the faces of Amarnian girls.

2

Foetuses of your womb, and my seed, lie in a farther room.
Spina bifida, one deformed, wrapped anyway with care
Swaddled like two little dolls in their Moses basket.

Love, our kitchens are tombs of such intimacy.

I restored the Theban Household of my father
Planned him building programmes, five-year estimates
For your gods; their temples, customs, your pious icons;
Allowed no proscription of the old, no persecution of the modern.

Piety's lavished on me from the five provinces;
You admire the grey wisdom of a youth of eighteen.
Eighteen! Eighteen! Shrines of generosity crowd my chambers.
Texts. Murals. My several hewn rooms you gift to the roof
        with odds and ends :

My sandals, my statues, my tunics and all the other likeables
I handled, or my fingers lately scented. I warm
        to the golden trumpets round my throne.

3

Mine is a nest of nests tears dry separately on,
The innermost of solid gold, the outer two of gold
Over cedar boughs. You load my arms with jewellery
And amulets. And you are lowering down my body
(It's a tight squeeze for priests, and the few I love).
For a living instant I embrace your earthly voices :
"His eyes are truly modelled. Time will surmise
The frail and graceful melancholy that was his."
And, then, there is the sealing and the silence.

A mote or two of dust lands on my sarcophagus
As empires and civilisations bloom and pass.
A rumour starts near Syria. Three men on trees.

Prophets overtaken by prophets. As thick as politicians
Miming opposite benches. When you lower the sound.
But adding to the honeyed droplets and the robbed
    and shattered combs.

4

I thank the gods for giving me this time –
So many are hauled out, resurrected for their message
Words rammed down their gullet for great purpose
And the building of distant panoplies and domes.

And so I lie on, wait beneath the stones.

In Egypt, as I grow tall,
The years hiss with revolution and anathemas
(Always the general Horemhab to restore order).
Above the moderate mind the very air has thinned.
People pack the temples with their fanatical open spaces.
Courtyards are linked by charismatic doors with broken lintels.

The desert grows intolerant of our fevered brows.
I seek what shade there is with lotus and papyrus.

Help me push out a frail rowboat in all of this.

5

Anarchy and a politic thigh fire the artists of Amarna.
Breasts are epicene; stomachs, slack; the shoulders, sloped.
I see faces lost to the paid romantics of the hour.
I'm fed into a Hittite War. Even as the universe widens.

When Carter and Craigavon snip off my fingers for the rings,
My penis for its diamond jewel, are you there at me too?
The forceps of a sterile science tugs at my epidermis.
I feel the rush of dry air, your dessicated energies.

This youthful mask! These gangling nextdoor bones!
My two front teeth are not your child's dental model.
Fragilities I loved fall apart now in other families.

This gold you'd touch is more, and less, than me.
Minor almost, I've never left my bridal teens.
So I'll not die, but sleep forever at eighteen.

SCHOOL YEAR START

I stand in at the red dairy door in my summer sandals.
They are polished fawn after the dust, the velvet pollen, of August.
I look across at the fed calves frisking down the Long Garden.
I touch that first white page, which opens to me in Irish :

"Mar chos an giorria do bhí mo chos" – limpid horizon.
The school book is vellum, pristine, the second day of September.
Warm. The sun is pure stasis. The deer on the page is in silhouette.
Wind fills the elm. The dry leaves ache and they are rustling.

Over in the house, the sound of willow plates stacked sideways
        on the dresser.
In the field, a first taking out of sheaves. Clatter of the blade.
Progress. My father is teaming the horses into their stride.
The runnels that drain our scented dairy are scoured and dry.
I drag the right sandal along the wide central one too long, too long.
I'm starting out again, and again must run the late mile
        to Cnoc-a-Bhile.

UNDER THE ELM

in memory of my mother

A gale-force March east south-easterly blows,
Dry enough to winnow the spring oats in.
Hat on, he is sweeping the cobble channel.
Saturday afternoon. Tidying time. Binder twine
Sheaves in his thoughts as the week winds down.
Scythe-edged cold. Difficulties as he tries to straighten :

I am sweeping the channel in his absence
(She will recount this scene for years on end)
I'm dressed for hardship, too, in his coat, felt hat.
She comes to the door for the washed potatoes,
Or to empty the full blue basin at the little gate?
I half turn, wave. See her heart begin to soar :
"For a minute I thought you were my daddy.
It was just that lift of the head you gave."

WILLOW PATTERN

She would lift you down for the dinner at Christmas,
The platter with the willow pattern shining all year,
Settle fir trees for the turkey on the December table.
Love birds up in the dresser air of a country house
Communed with each other, wing tip to wing tip,
Hovered above Earle's bridge across the stream.

We sat together all spring, summer, autumn, winter.
Yet on that day only we gazed down on fir tops.

Delft, deflt grew cracked like a desert wadi
Over half a century on the warm family table
Dwindling every year like a thought of wings,
A bridge to cross in the heavens, boyhood's firs
Consumed in a three-day holocaust. Givers, receivers,
We were all alive, well, around home those days.

IN MEMORY OF JOHN GOWRAN

grandfather

They would have burned your house to the ground
Because you told them to their faces what they were.
They had gathered to execute the cold details
With blackened cheeks, without shame or fear.

Sons of maimers. Thieves. Men who stole from widows.
Pews were hewn for them and their Mass-hatted wives.
I saw them genuflect, manoeuvre into seats, bent over
Fingering at devotions their remorseless black beads.

Ideals. They never knew them. Neither the word nor the concept.
Yet their tight offerings could grace stained glass and trancept.

Small men. Small deaths still flaming their bald pallid skulls:
Incense of thatch. Incense of terror. Old fears. Old fires instilled.

Sordid men. Insurgents of a kind you despised.
Lionised with the years. Romanticised.

THE RING

mother, after the troubles

I think of its shining in the earth
Like some fabulous leaven in the soil.
Its worn gold in the long night will warm the clay
And your tender finger reduced to bone.

I remember how we'd to wait outside St. James's
Locked mortuary for the undertakers to eat their dinner.
Urchins sat on the high walls in the brewery stench
Vultures ready to swoop. Break in, whip off the ring

If we turned the head.
None guarded the dead
In the blazing September of twenty-one when he took
You, at eighteen, to Dublin for the honeymoon.

The ring gleamed, then, in the morning, hadn't yet slimmed with toil
As you washed in the sun by jug and wash basin in a tumbled room,
Shone in a gutted city where he'd found an hotel for bride and groom.

MONTBRETIA SUNDAY

This is Cemetery Sunday with montbretia, your old dahlias,
Our graves are a mass of Coralstown blooms and wreaths.
Plots are dug, raked, tidied or sheared over to the last.
From the August church you can see Heathstown.

O yes, Assumption Day when the clay that covers
The deep-piled bones comes alive, throbs with reds, purples and blues;
When dead mothers, daughters, sons and fathers
Have salt-spiked water shaken over them while the living
        pay their dues.

And I remember my own father and mother, too,
And theirs before them. It's years since they went down.
They're just poor bones now and the elm wood that hid them
        from our final view
Has weakened, let the gradual clay settle in about their temples
        moist and brown.

Assumption Mother, I see you sit next to Peter's well.
Photo call. On your lap a baby. My story still to tell.

THE KNIFE

He has stormed in to get the knife.
The black boning knife that cut through pig carcasses
Lusted after the scythestone to gleam and plunge with a tapered edge.
He has been fattening the old cow to clear debt
And she is no heavier, she's no heavier in his eyes.
He has been stallfeeding her and his calculating hands have skimmed
Her thighs daily, firmed the flesh, but not to bruise. He is in a rage.
Speech has deserted him on the wasting animal.

He has stormed in for the knife in the rattling drawer
(Ill in bed, out of March primary, I hear it all)
And they wonder why, ask him in the fifties kitchen.
Hoarsely he whispers, 'I will put an end to her, put an end
To her'. I hear them wrestle with him crying for the knife, hear
Despair and unpaid bills in their voices and his voice,
        too, too far gone for tears.

VALLEYS OF THE VACANT WINDOWS

There was the dawn, too, when you stopped.
When the heart seemed to go out of you.
Even if you went through the fierce emotions
Of tackle and harness, the orchard clearings.

You that were first with gleaming machines
To meet the market, eager tomes on tillage
From the ministry, their fulfilled analyses.
Pounds, shillings, pence, blue faded ink.

For the dark years came and the church gaters.
Brand new ascendency. Looking into their soul
They sensed opportunity, the salient economic.
While the knackers moved off with your cattle.

So it was, round the thirteen thousand died.
Even if their windows were not yet your eyes.

ENTERPRISE

The business was timed to a Sunday nicety.
Gaelic supporters in the turnstyle. Say, two or three –
"Will you buy me the ticket?" Tug at your sleeve.
"Because I've only a shilling, or so, on me."

At the very style, jostled, hemmed in with the others
He'd turn. Annoyance smoothed his moustache. "Did your mother
Hand you no money at all coming out for the game?"
"Well, she did give me, she did give me, some".

The ticket dispenser would make no virtue of patience.
I'd be into Cusack Park, her half-crown to the good.
He'd forget the ritual whether the ball was in or not with helloes
As we picked our path through knees to a place on a bench.

Till half-time struck up with pipeband and Dublin fruitsellers.
He'd remember. "C'mon, you'll fork out now for two apples".

I knew the change in my pocket would be warm with her silver.
The sun shone on my curls like the colour of jerseys, of cheers.

ILLUMINATION

The cart is stacked with sheaves for the haggard,
    the ropes are stretched taut
and knotted at the base of the shafts. In the mountain field, the height
that gave a view of Wicklow crests, the terrier barks less
    in the flattened circle
of stubble that was a sheaf stack. He snags the mother mouse down
    in one gulp.
His paw uncovers – or is it the gleaming pitchfork? – the clean
    chaffy nest with four
baby mice, pink, hairless and delicate, faintly moving,
    where a furrow home
ran lately with breeding spaces and the curves of oats divided in gold
once at the end of August in a warm wind when the idea
    of a home was considered.

After the barking, the laughing, the shouting, the last stack,
    they are looking down, three of
my brothers from their cargo of corn. Astride the sheaves
    in uncustomary silence. The full moon rises
over O'Hara's. Oval as a face and still, pure orange. The cart creaks,
    sways away into the twilight.

Your faces have grown pale. A wind stirs. Hint of later frost?
    Mist? Fog at daybreak?
The threshing's near. I linger by the quiet forms a half-hour or more
    till I am called.
On my hunkers under a clear October night. The last to walk away
    from the nest.

THIS CHURCH
THAT IS STRIPPED DOWN

"There is the empty chapel, only the wind's home."

T. S. Eliot, *The Wasteland*

"And you must go inland and be
Lost in compassion's ecstasy,
Where suffering soars in summer air –
The millstone has become a star."

Patrick Kavanagh, *Prelude*

VISITING CHRIS KIELY
AT THE J.F.K. ARBORETUM

I walk through the gleaming corridor
Marbled with the history of the genera.
All is mid-day peace, red cedarwood.

And in your office, well-stocked as a nursery,
Are shelves and shelves of volumes on trees.
O forests within forests of conceptual care.

You intimate this to be the least of the seasons.
Yet I confess I love this November leaflessness,
The essence that beckons of trees outside in bud
A people woken, excitement at their fingertips,
            in some passover manifest.

The weeping ash is jubilant, mature in its twig-drooped tendrils
And if the tulip tree's gone lemon, loathe to shed its Tibetan leaves
The eucalypti at New Ross are stripping down to a white nakedness.
Their boles are vulnerable. They're shedding old habits
            in their stride.

LEMONGROVE

Collar on, and the black hat, in those days of vacation
I drove to your father's funeral over at Lemongrove.
The church was unlocked for the hymned occasion.
I remember the damp, like the wheezing harmonium,

Seep far into my teenage bones. I sat in a back pew.
I had walked proudly in the old mossy gate, glad to leave
Locals gawking on the outside. They feared the nape-raising
    "Which" for "Who".
I saw nobody to bridge the wintry gap in the nave.

You cut meadows in my primary years after the horses went
In Gallstown, Woodville, Drumman and Claremont.

My father talked long with yours of cattle and government
Over hedges that were a treat on mornings to the turfbank.

So, Billy, I'd come over to pay my respects. Again to say hello.
You gripped my hand so hard, I wondered when you'd let it go.

TO THE CONSIDERATE DEAD

circa mid C17th

1

Your names are not emblazoned on our hearts,
Survive only as milder curios in their passing,
Fire the belly of neither revolutionary nor defender,
Neither insurrection script, nor the hyperbole of deliverance.
Defenders of a neighbour's patch, your minds'
Innocence inclines to waywardness, fleece on barbed wire.
You've common names like those found on cafes, pubs, dog licences.

If you'd known our streets, you'd have stood at a neighbour's door,
Absorbing the bullet that pierces the warmth of kitchens
Speeds the draughty hallways, landings and the darkness,
Smashes the ply of partitions, beds, awkward passions.
Your long foolhardy silence has been golden, to some purpose.
Your heaven is removed from ours that's ensilaged to eternity.
Your names are like old doors that groan, do not properly close.

2

Straddling our divides, you do not totally scare.
Sanctuary and buttermilk are offered in your houses,
Bread under eaves and in corners where the dour sects sulk.
While we clear families and tables, scour for arms
You keep your counsel. Your adrenalin may cool to ice
Still you persevere, owe no allegiance to titular cities.
Your orchards are early. Out of the way. Open to frost.

Sometimes you beckon, open to us in the sun on vistas
Of August heather, dry sphagnum, all those certainties
That send up the fresh cankered bud to feed our sickness.
Ethnic deliverance. The spluttering over more graves.
If decency is debased coinage to the face of faction
You know the scene intimately, are tested in heat.
Crafted like golden bowls, you will forever gleam.

3

No curias, or kirks, will promote your bony cause
The cross, furious grumbling of your welcomes.
The thousand intolerances of the cutaway bog
We are heirs to, so ready to quake under all,
Swallow us with exhausted pogroms, who'll
Make new obeisance to new herded madness,
Forge concord with the victors of old insolence.

You have common names. Like those found on cafes. Pubs.
   Dog licences.
I would wear your lost relics, like old talismans,
If I could find them. For yours could be the earth
Whatever critical, tolerant fields we might-re-seed.
Creators of short drives. Paths with mute poplars.

Over you
No heads bow, or place flowers commemorial and fresh.
Come, wreathe our briary hearts, so tribal and dead.

THE FAR EAST

I sat on the partition seat with the long cushion in aunt Kate's kitchen
opening the Far East covers with the placid waters of
        the piled monthlies.
Solitary with sails the languid sampan moved on a river wider
        than the Shannon.

Odd stories tumbled from the pages of the pens of missionaries
        to tingle the spine :
a mountain people laughing at the death of their loved ones
        to our priests,
crying their fill at weddings and across the laden trestles
        of celebration.

Communists, one summer month, swept south like a million
        Ghengis Khans
flaming the wooden fifties churches of the Maynooth
        Mission to China.
I moved to the table for tea and jam on the bread aboard
        the graceful sampan.
Then back to the porch partition for pudsy ryan as Kate's fowl
        complained in the doorway.

Mostly I remember that man on the water plying the oar as if
        with an hour to spare
while eddies of missionaries milled in his wake to bring him,
        like Confucius,
tidings of a greater joy, till it was time to walk home,
        by the deserted cross,
Cnoc-a-Bhile, gathering place through invasions no youths
        flocked to anymore.

THE LOST HONEY

'91/'92

August and the mostly dry combs of wax are stored in their barrels,
Extracted with little or no liquid honey, while the transistor
Is agog with the failed coup in Moscow and Yeltsin climbs
Up onto the tank to talk to the world and that plain man, John Major.

April and the loft's white combs are re-aired and the old guard
Are brushed away like sly drones cowering in empty corners.
Above in the apiary, the weakest hives are robbed. Syrup feed
      is useless.
Hives are consumed. Old satellites. Christ, no end to horror.

Moths and their maggots slept in combs though the barrels lay sealed.
I check the supers again for any weakness, hammer more bright nails.

So many hours are frittered in hope. The loft hoard is near empty,
I go up and down the blessed ladder. The day's climbing is endless.

Boris has been denied his absolute power. Good. Hope here,
Too, on the periphery? Stocks are divided. I see promise
      gild the oilseed rape.

85

LADIES IN STONE

i.m. S. Plath d. 11 Feb. '63

We will make use of your blue statuary down the years,
Conceived like any girl in times of war turbulence and tears,
Life ahead of you, in you, lithe and sexual, with a mind of your own.
You walk alone to Elizabeth the cruel sixty miles of crosses

Revolution stinks on. In the garden your proud relentless hives
    turn to stone.
Relatives sit round like iron. Iron in their gaze. In their hearts.
Juda boulders in that far hill country are London furnaces.
Craftsmen fume for words in a steam over mid-day gruel.

I remember you both now, one just as white as the other.
    And as cold and as blue.
At the Lourdes Grotto our young hairy wrists froze
    with morning numbness.
Our fingers were cavitied with chilblains. On our knees
    the Galway black
Of our novitiate lives whitened in the thin eastern snow.

Ladies in stone, look down on us today with what grace
    you can muster,
Free of the bleak eyes of men. And women. Our tears for the cold.
    Our ineffectual stare.

HANG BY ME

That You should love, that I know You love, me
As part of your blessed store is beyond belief.
Paradise is in your glance, this near intimacy,
As I hang by your side. I'm "the good thief":

Some gather now to break both my legs, for it is
The custom in this City. I wait on for the blow,
The excruciating pain can't be worse than your loss.
And from your tender side, too, blood begins to flow

With secretions that make up more of You.
And that I dared to open my lips at all shocks me.
I had long gone into numbness. O nothing new.
My hand stretches out to yours above the scoffers' mockery.

Friend of friends, I suffocate. Give me fresh air.
You know at the end, too, only an intimate despair.

A MEMORY OF EMMAUS

They have gone back again to their floodlit temples,
To the darker recesses and the altars of stone.
What god in his right senses would want to live in such places?

They have gone back, again, to their floodlit temples,
To the murmurs of offering, incense and ersatz,
Young priests in their element with goblets of gold.

They have gone back, again, to their floodlit temples.
The breaking of bread was not enough for their mouths
In a pub, in a restaurant, or with us by a good fire.

They have gone back, again, to their floodlit temples.
The Mother & Child and the Egypt-bound father in roseate
Glass are a lie to the exile, the slavework they knew:

You would not have asked, ever, for our tall stupid spires,
Who saw at the table the one nod, or two nods, of tenderness to her
        over the years
Of coupled hurt till tears were transfigured to a new resin
        when You were found.
That long consolation of limbs when they knew You were around.

REFLECTION, CÉLI DÉ

c. C8th

If You were not, I doubt if I could love.
I can say I never knew affection
Till You passed by the shore, or destitution of
Everything I hold closest, every earthly satisfaction,

When You were not to be followed in the dunes, spoken to.
And everything that has passed for love has been false –
The routine and the tinsel, the crude, the tribal view
That tolls in its cold, eclectic souls. And little else.

You alone stand for my mountain, my sustenance.
You give my soul bread with the young ravens.
You watch over my slippery steps with your glance.
You've given me gifts, cleared the night heavens

Of my mind when nothing but the gales blew there
On crooked thorn, and rocks, with saltspray bitter everywhere.

CÉLI DÉ IN HIBERNATION

I am in the season of dormancy
And rest and will not be disturbed so
Do not attempt to raise the sap in me.
It is not the season when love should grow.

My life now is so much gone into stone
It would take damn near all of your Younge Sunne to warm
The veins where the mica shows alone.
There is no sense in your coming to harm.

Let me be, then, to wander the bracken waste,
The mountain ridges with the occasional
Snows on the heath, to walk on in haste
If I please, or slow down to the final crawl.

No embrace will save me from this pit.
The higher I climb to You, the deeper I sink into it.

RESPONSE TO A YOUNG CÉLI DÉ

I am the bright ripples touched off in the universe.
In as many rationalities as will fit on the pins
Of a galaxy of Gribbins, the mere gossip of Science.
I thrill with each supernova that blows at the last kiss of its days.

A whisker out in the properties, and you'd have no call on me;
I set your coincidences in lovely motion once, so take heart.
What is a billion years to you and to our affection?
I follow your everyday parable down the Milky Way.

For if the simple death of a star gives birth to another,
You are the bud of a dead genius in another universe.
I breathed on you and you on me, once, in a starry nursery.
Love me. In a moment of simplicity, I brought you to
        my boundless house.

Give thanks, then, for what your face wrests from the sun,
O happy youth of air, and carbon, and iron.

KAVANAGH'S OLD HORSE

1

It will in the end be like this for most of us
A place with clean sheets, or pasture, a bonus
Thankfulness ebbing like a tide that will not come in again,
A spot perhaps among old docks, thistles and plantain
Talkative in their last seed and just as anxious.
Maybe a crab in bloom, or setting to bitter fruit,
Or that mellowing time on headland grasses for winter rodents.

Black crows will pass by curious in themselves
But our spirit for them is not yet ready carrion.
Maybe seagulls, too, our way will be blown in
White and starchy in their flight from our ills.
Maybe someone will place a cool palm on our brow
As we whisper a name of diminishing syllables.
But our heads, by then, will have grown quite heavy and stupid.

2

Children with primrose faces on the banks round our beds –
Or coming and going to the hospital shop for more sweets –
Yes, the real world will go on in the yards between our sheets.
A visitor, at last, will nod in our direction. We will have grown tired
Of answering. Too late for us, then, to murmur old litanies
Of yarrow and daisy, of cynical ragwort, mild sowthistle,
Primula Veris where artificial is unknown. Columcille,

Poor horse, I thought of you both tonight when I heard
Old men gostering on the stairs of Ballybricken chapel
The boys finding merriment in their dotage, ramblings.

So we leave things as we found them, the blackbird
Defining nobody's territory, a nest or two to survive,

The ragwort, broken, withered, scoffing at our side
Adoring forever in the one true church of the fields.

THE GENTLE PALM
MUSE COUNTRY II

"See, I have branded you on the palms of my hands."

Isaiah, 49, 15 & 16

DIARMUID TO FIONN

Wise one, I've been lying low here all day
Crying "Water! Water!" Hoping for your quick return.
You bring me just enough to see me slip away.
You have me prostrate the way you want. My fevers burn.

My blood and other matter flow apart from me
Staunched by their own excess and deeper want.
I have a view of fields, boar hunting to the sea.
I thought we were friends again, that you'd haunt

My vulnerable sleep no more. Gráinne, who chose
Me, do you still so covet her for all I've done?
Educator, I pass out under the bee-laden dogrose.
You leave me, for food, last week's rancid bone.

I go the way that most boar go. Frothing.
Delayed? Again? What's in your palms? Nothing?

A FATHER TO SON

I measure out my love for you in far too few embraces
Of the human, like when you came to me from the tomb
Found her clinging hands a burden, the familiar faces
At their gossip at the planting. Then the golden harvest in the womb.

And I have waited all eternity, and before it, just for this –
To see you on the mountain and in the river with the water
Glistening on your flowing locks, with John, before the kiss
Of Salomé would take him with a taste for slaughter

Up in the courts. But you have kept his orphic head
And I send you down again, and again, so that I
Might have you wake them up from the dead.
Gather them with the wheatfields of immortality.

So I will embrace your love whenever I can,
Know your godlike joy in woman and in man.

AERIAL

This is the airport of your departure words.
You wisely put off till the last the final choice.
Names now slide fast by the eye. Craft wait like birds
To fly you anywhere, to those inner crowded shores
　　or pure fields of shining ice.

There is the taxiing and the taking off
The banking into blue, the first brush with cloud.
New skies, new countries are yours. Names to rhyme and love.
Your heart is free at last. Your wings are proud.

You have survived another year and so you climb,
Soon feel the clayey earth fall farther from your feet :
You are tracking across the lanes of Icarus and time.
The sky is lucid blue. Your spirit skips a beat,

Maybe, for at this swift and cruising altitude all
Is possible, both the glorious earthly and the magisterial.

BÉCQUER FORGIVES

The deft swallow in you now will soon return,
The dark and graceful swallow of my dream.
I'll watch you build your nest and learn
Of tenderness again, your wing close to his as you both climb

Blue skies for insects and stop a second in the air.
You savour your flight and his until twilight, or rain,
Forces you down between the honeysuckle. Too fragrant, too fair,
This is grief, to hear your wing no more upon my window pane.

While I write, the heavy dews fall soft and slow.
Let these notes of mutual forgiveness be ours
Thudding in my vitals like the hammer blows
They are. Through your sleeping hours

My body aches. On you two may love be unguent,
Whom the twittering summer days have joined.

QUANDO FIAM CEU CHELIDON

Young bird of flight, we all root for your grace
On wings, to leave so far below all this pollution,
The muds and mires that suck us down in disgrace.
We'd rise higher and higher still toward the sun

Of a fine August day when the insect kingdom
Is flying high too and every blessed thing
Is thankful for cloudlessness, the blue crumb.
Around us our brothers and our sisters sing.

They are as near to, and as far from, us as that.
We weave and curve, then bank, slide and dive
Hours that are eternities. On the flat
Fields below men trade, argue, fight and die. Alive, alive

They never were, tasted our rapture at this height.
Yet we must return to their warm stables, rest there every night.

THE OPEN PALM

I am cupped these days in your gentle palms.
I am not able to, yet might, be free.
I it was that sought refuge there from harm.
Your gentle fingers have these months nested me

Back to strength, vision, plumage, colour. You've been kind;
I've felt your fond fingers stroke me back to life,
Your lips caress my eyes, your cheeks, my mind.
I stirred once, my claws gripped your skin. I was alive.

And if now you feel my wings strain
And I grow uneasy for other skies,
My home, I must dare out into the pain
Of flight, the criss-crossed hawk immensities.

And know however far this flight is, I will but circle you.
Come back, like the migrant will, seek out your palms anew.

FRAGILITY

What is that winged heart beating on about?
You know its secret, maybe, better than itself
Could ever imagine, its terror that will out,
Or its eyes glaze back in and close, beyond help.

What is that fragile heart so on about? It
Beats faster, faster in its drive for flight.
It's so afraid, that bird, it may well shit
Itself, it's so limed and ringed in its plight.

See, when you open your palms, how slow
It is to leave your friendship and your love.
You hold it high, then, on open palms as Francis would
        years ago.
And yet it does not move. It does not move.

It must have some message for you before it flies.
A message you can only guess at from its eyes.

SKEPTIKOS

You taught us once such openness in flight
We dared to clear the houses, muddy yards:
We're in the air as never before. Our fright
Is palpable. Will you pick up the shards

If we falter or are blasted from the air?
Will you protect us from the cold fortune
Hunters, will you shield us from their stare
When they sense victory, will you be the one

To gather up the disabled pieces of our life
When there's nothing but shot-riddled plumage?
Will you harbour our chicks in all this strife?
We once followed a vision, it was no mirage.

We wander now the far dark and stony places,
Heights bereft of your love, bereft of your embraces.

ASH

See how light now my bones rest on your palm.
This is, my friend, the end of evolution and of dreams.
The end of swamps, depressions, each bleak triassic calm,
The end of all vulnerable creatures who ate by rivulets and streams

Awkward in thought and huge in movement. Great of eye.
I have long known, carried you within me
Until this day when I put you finally by
Shedding you like all notions of eternity.

My wings and all, they are near weightless now
For this is as near flight as I can ever be.
I cling to your finger like to a brittle bough.
I'll vanish if you breathe down hard on me.

Keep me a little longer in your view
As I hold you eye to eye to praise you.

CARAVAN

Will we survive, then, in the tiny flock
That graces blue April and autumn dawns,
Like communes of the higher airs, though gales rock
Their forest trees, at one time to lay bare crowns

Of golds, reds and mauves, at another
To emphasise the bare despairing arms
Men call branches, they so flail about for all the bother
We're heirs to? Who believe in summer more than anyone believes.

We will feed on pastures where we can,
The lugworm ricegrass shores, the saltmarshes of the mind,
Then quickly rise to take off at the sound of man
Fearful of his ratrace and his caged kind.

So roam like plover, brent geese, or the ptarmigan
Whose home is the chancy sky, the high outcast V, the lofty caravan.

SAN JUAN DE LA CRUZ CONSIDERS SOLITUDE

You are passing beyond me and I
Cannot hold you. You are flying across
Seas and the simian nations at peace now while I
Know only turbulence and in my racing skull the start of moss.

I have no wings to catch you. The very thought
Is so ridiculous. Yet I know if
I do not reach you the rot
Will set in on me profoundly, leave me stiff.

I would be counselled by cabbages and kings.
Soul, mad man, I see no hope of living out my days.
I will set my affections in order, divide my things
Among those who were my good friends always.

I have battered my heart alone asleep.
And yet I still have promises to keep.

MOSAIC

You said our only home is timelessness,
Or thereabouts; it is quite near the mountains
And we have wandered down the slopes to dress
With wonderment the chestnut trees in summer rains.

We miss the blue hills of now, the summit ledge,
Caught as we are in the grind of animal and mire,
But we too have kept fast that fragrant pledge
Strayed with our love into mosaics of fire.

And we will be seen by others, who will scoff –
Those that put paid fences about birth and death
To barbwire us all in. We will not have it in our love –
We'll come out from the fires ennobled, in good health.

But for us the day is going and the sun is cold with showers.
And we have as little space, as little hope, within the hours.

FAMILY

You go from love. You will come back to love.
For in my house are many rooms, those mansions
Some have written of, enough space for daughters, sons
And friends of friends in the bright rooms above

Open to a view of apples, pears, all types of fruit,
Edenic sustenance that ripens in your golden absence.
If you need to sleep, to rest, that space will be private.
Have no fear, the only voices will be of innocence

Contending with the green choirs not yet laid bare :
The clear mistle thrush on the top branch of a spruce;
The blackbirds hungry, honey-beaked, single, in pairs,
The white owl vying with the full moon for limpid space.

Creation will be evident. You will know harmony
Like a beat well regulated within the heart. An inner sea.

PRAYER FOR MY SONS

Well, my prayer is that you will always know
The daily rebirth of affection and of love.
I believe that out of your side new trees will grow
To shed ardour with no tinge of leaves in a grove.

And not just love for yourself, Emmet, Jonathan
For that would be too one-dimensional,
But in and for another's graceful hands
Embracing you, then, in a mirrored hall.

And may deep springs pour freely in your house,
Your hands enclose for good a pair of doves
Whose griefs will rest lightly. So, let you rouse
Love to old mediterranean heights. If olive

Dawns, the Song of Songs you'll know by heart,
             compose a better hymn
Than mine to love with each final paroxysm.

WHEN THE POETRY'S OVER

Poetry's a steadfast friend until the end.
Dear girl, it's now almost half a century
Since you first touched my palm, gave all you could lend
Of toys and themes, soulful things to humour me.

You were my love as teenager, in torn adolescence.
You were my guardian in the slick, black, trusted years.
You helped me re-construct my life, make some sense
Of this last score. You're the sole one I can confide my fears

To. Sister, who is not sister, wife, close one, daily friend,
Confidant all the days. You've not failed me when it mattered.
When I pick up the pen, you take the other hand,
Explain why we are so, why all our likes, and loves lie scattered.

And if I will one day fail you, understand,
I tried. Tried to hold onto your firm, tender, hand.

VEDIC

Let all our future poems be dying swans
And may Lilia Musovarova rule them all
As they come on stage for our loved ones:
Let them be, in the main, at their beck and call,

Choreograph the daily griefs, dramas, joys, the little harms
And let them know our love for them is sound :
We that have known the ripple and the wingspan in the arms
The attempts at flight that never leave the ground.

Let us incorporate grace, at once balletic and proud,
The courage of the solo in the words of every poem,
The dancing essences to be soft spoken, or cried aloud,
Fearless of nothing but the loss of those bright waters we call home.

And may these failing birds find resurrection in our wills
Retrace their wings to cignethood on lakes between the hills.